I Found Him...

Mrs. Roy,

    May you find our extraordinary God in ordinary places.

                      Jeff Jenkins

I FOUND HIM...

Reflections of God's Presence

Jeff Jenkins

DEDICATION

To Boyce Gire, whose energy, enthusiasm, and passion for life were contagious. Throughout his life, and during his battle with ALS, he inspired many by his positive attitude, which permeated from his unwavering faith. Boyce enriched lives simply by being himself; as a teacher, father, grandfather, son, husband, and friend.

CONTENTS

CONTENTS

ACKNOWLEDGMENTS

To my wife, Bedie, for riding the back roads with me looking for unusual photographic shots and whose feedback, creativity, and enthusiasm are greatly appreciated. To my friends who continue to encourage and inspire me when I have doubts. To my children, Leigh and Jay, for simply being great kids. To my brothers and sisters and their families for their unconditional love; and to all of the Facebook friends who "Follow", "Share", "Comment" and "Like" these posts; THANK YOU!

WWW.Facebook.com/IFoundHimMinistry

Spring

I FOUND HIM...BLUEBIRD

A bluebird perched on a budding tree limb shouts that spring is indeed approaching. The long dark dreary days of winter will soon fade away giving birth to renewed life. Dormant plants will appear reborn, the air will be filled with the sounds of singing birds, and a revived spirit of energy will prevail. What a wonderful time of year!

During this spring season, as life appears to emerge from the dead of winter, let us consider what season it is for us in our lives. The beautiful verses in Ecclesiastes 3 poetically tell us that "there is a season, and a time to every purpose under the heaven…"

While observing buds blooming and grass greening, be reminded of Easter; the greatest rebirth imaginable. Think of Titus 3:4-6 "But when the kindness and love of God our Savior appeared, he saved us, not because of righteous things we had done, but because of his mercy. He saved us through the washing of rebirth and renewal by the Holy Spirit, whom he poured out on us generously through Jesus Christ our Savior".

Maybe this changing season is a time to reevaluate our lives, our purpose, and our priorities. Maybe the renewed energy of spring will renew our focus. Maybe it is indeed our season to follow His lead, discern His will, and strive each day to please Him, not us.

I Found Him…as a beautiful bluebird rested from his busy day.

I FOUND HIM...BABY RABBIT

A baby rabbit, only weeks old, hides under a shrub, petrified by something foreign, unknown; a human with a camera. His instinct is to lay low, blend in, and not be noticed. Fear of the new experience drives him to seek camouflage, hoping that the intruder is unaware and will vanish.

The rabbit is simply following his instinct; his survival mechanism. Humans face similar challenges. Maybe not as dramatic as being stalked by an unknown figure; but nevertheless, daunting situations arise at work, at home, and in normal living. We can hide like the rabbit, or we can have the confidence that God is with us, helping us, guiding us, leading us. Psalms 62:7 says "My protection and success come from God alone. He is my refuge, a Rock where no enemy can reach me."

What a difference Faith makes. Yes, we have "butterflies"; yes, we are apprehensive with new situations; and yes, we do fear the unknown. People of Faith, however, understand and believe the words written in Psalms 62: 1-2 "I stand silently before the Lord, waiting for Him to rescue me. For salvation comes from Him alone. Yes, He alone is my Rock, my rescuer, defense and fortress. <u>Why then should I be tense with fear when troubles come?</u>"

Unlike the fearful baby rabbit, we can boldly face our challenges, knowing that He alone is our Rock.

I Found Him...in the eyes of a baby rabbit.

I FOUND HIM...ABANDONED STOREFRONT

This building seems to shout "I was once the center of attention; a destination. People thought of me, came to me, told their friends about me. Now I'm forgotten and abandoned."

Can these same words not be spoken by God himself regarding the manner in which He has been abandoned by some? Having a relationship with God is just that; a relationship. It requires work, effort, and ongoing maintenance. Certainly loving and following Him one day only to ignore Him on another is not the answer. The relationship needs nurturing, just as this once vibrant store needs ongoing maintenance.

Time gradually separates some from the Lord. It's easy to skip prayer, worship, and time with the Lord. The easy path in hectic lives is one without God. It's an earthly path, and one with grave consequences. As stated in Psalms 73 "… I came so close to the edge of the cliff! My feet were slipping and I was almost gone. For I was envious of the prosperity of the proud and wicked. Yes, all through life their road is smooth…Why take the trouble to be pure…" Later in the text, the consequences are revealed. "Their present life is only a dream. They will awaken to the truth…" But for the faithful, Psalms 73 states "You will keep on guiding me all my life…and receive me into the glories of heaven".

I Found Him…in the decaying walls of a once bustling store.

Jeff Jenkins

I FOUND HIM...PEONY

A peony, in full bloom, reaches its full potential as sunlight softly bounces off its petals. What a sight! Off to the side, not quite in focus, is a bud. Not yet in bloom, it patiently waits for its time.

We, like the peony, are made up of several parts. Just as we have arms, legs, eyes and ears, which make up our body; God graciously has bestowed upon each of us spiritual gifts, each equally important, to make up the Body of His Kingdom. Gifts include compassion, leadership, teaching, shepherding, intercession/prayer, administration, and many others. 1 Corinthians 12:27 states: "...All of you together are the one body of Christ and each of you is a separate and necessary part of it".

Many of us have not yet realized that we indeed do have gifts; and thus these God-given gifts are underutilized. Just as the bud has not blossomed, neither have we in our work for the Lord. The potential is there, the gift is in place. Maybe, just maybe, it is our time. Summer is approaching; is now the time to shine? The bud does not fully bloom instantly, it takes time. The same with us; nourish the bud, allow it to grow. There is a gorgeous flower hiding in there; and God is calling us to let it bloom.

I Found Him...in the bud of a peony.

I FOUND HIM...CARDINAL

I watched birds maneuver around a backyard bird feeder during a recent snow. Cardinals, blackbirds, and a woodpecker all looked on patiently from strategic points as sparrows dominated the feeder. Over time, they all ate.

Contrast this to our everyday lives. Think of our reactions to an extra-long stop light, a somewhat slow moving cashier, or to a computerized help desk when we simply want to speak to a human. Consider our reactions with family, friends, neighbors, co-workers and strangers that act contrary to our wishes.

The Bible instructs us to be patient. James 5:7-8 for example, says "...Be patient then brothers, until the Lord's coming. See how the farmer waits for the land to yield its valuable crop and how patient he is for the autumn and spring rains. You too, be patient, and stand firm, because the Lord's coming is near". God is certainly patient with us. Simon Peter tells us in 2 Peter 3:8 "...With the Lord a day is like a thousand years, and a thousand years are like a day...He is patient with you, not wanting anyone to perish, but everyone to come to repentance."

Think about giving the gift of patience to loved ones, acquaintances, as well as to strangers. Withhold judgment, accept them as they are, and allow them to grow. God is giving us time, we can do the same for others.

I Found Him, observing hungry birds share a snow covered feeder.

I FOUND HIM...WILD ONION

In this picture of a wild onion, the camera is focused on the plant, with everything else blurred out. This technique encourages the viewer to see what the photographer intends and makes for a dramatic image without clutter.

Certainly in life, the ability to focus on what is important and to "blur-out" distractions is a wonderful trait. Often times we focus on the insignificant and ignore what's important. God intends for us to love Him, worship Him, focus on Him, and not get side-tracked. This is a FULL-TIME job. It is very tempting and too easy to focus on earthly distractions; money, possessions, status, looks, etcetera. Tread carefully, these are fools-gold.

Psalms 37:23-24 tells us that "The steps of good men are directed by the Lord. He delights in each step we take. If they fall it isn't fatal, for the Lord holds them with His hands." So the lesson is simple, not necessarily easy, but simple. Trust in the Lord; discern His will; FOCUS ON HIM. Just as a photographer focuses on the subject, we too should focus (refocus) our lives, seeing the long-term will of God while minimizing the distractions that simply confuse the picture. David continues in Psalms 37: 27-28 "So if you want an eternal home, leave your evil, low-down ways and live good lives. For the Lord loves justice and fairness; He will never abandon his people."

Focus—on the Lord.

I Found Him...while looking at a wild onion.

I FOUND HIM...NESTING BIRD

It is truly amazing what one sees when looking through the lens of a camera. Details often taken for granted come to life. This determined bird sits, day after day, patiently nurturing four eggs. Bees buzz while working a flower, birds are hunting, buds are blooming, hornets feverishly build a fortress, spiders engineer amazing webs, squirrels are busily stealing nuts, and butterflies flit from flower to flower. Sunrises, sunsets, fog, dew, the moon and stars, even the clouds all come alive; if we simply slow down and quietly look and listen. What a show is performed daily!

In Psalms 104, David praises God, His Kingdom and all that He created. He beautifully describes God's creation, all of its intertwined parts; indeed life itself.

In the hectic rush to survive another day, it is easy to ignore the beauty around us. We forget the complexity of God's total Kingdom. A great healing exercise is to slow down; look, listen, smell, touch, and just observe. Prayer naturally evolves.

David continues in Psalms 104:31 "Praise God forever! How He must rejoice in all of His work!" And in verses 33-34 "I will sing to the Lord as long as I live. I will praise God to my last breath. May He be pleased by all of these thoughts about Him, for He is the source of all my joy".

Slow down, ponder His omnipotent power, and thank Him.

I Found Him… as a bird faithfully tended to her eggs.

I FOUND HIM…WEATHERVANE

An antique weathervane sits high atop a tall steeple, doing its job; changing as the wind changes. Although this has been a valuable tool for centuries, it is ironic that so many people appear to mimic its role. Does it not remind you of people who change their beliefs and their direction seemingly as often as the wind shifts? They are easily lead astray because they have no clear-cut direction in their lives. These people, as do we all, need an additional tool; one that is solid, firm, and steadfast. We need one that will not change with each new fad, one that stands the test of time, and one that never wears out. We NEED the Lord!

The Bible is the "tool" that enlightens us on God's straight and steady course. In verse after verse, chapter after chapter, the Bible sets the course. Psalms 119:2 for example: tells us: "Happy are all who search for God, and always do His will, rejecting compromise with evil, and <u>walking only in His paths</u>." Again in verse 133: "<u>Guide me</u> with Your laws so that I will not be overcome by evil." Jeremiah's prayer in Jeremiah 10:23 explains it well: "I know, O Lord, that a man's life is not his own; it is not for man to direct his steps…."

Stay the course. Allow the Word of God, through the Holy Spirit, to guide you.

I Found Him…in the ever-turning arm of an antique weathervane.

I FOUND HIM...CHIPPING SPARROW

I watched a Chipping Sparrow perched on a tree during a recent snow. He primarily forages on the ground for insects and seeds, pouncing on worms and such. On this day, he seemed very patient in that his typical hunting area, the ground, was covered with snow.

We too wake up to surprises that throw us out of our normal routines. Often times our plans are altered due to unforeseen events. We get frustrated when people; family, friends, co-workers or even strangers simply do not act as we want. Our patience is worn thin.

Paul speaks to this in 2 Corinthians 6 when he describes the hardships that his ministry endured. In spite of being beaten, thrown in jail, enduring sleepless nights and going without food, they persevered. In verse 6 he says that they remain "in purity, understanding, patience and kindness; in the Holy Spirit and in sincere love". Paul also tells us in Galatians 5:22 that the fruit of the spirit is, among other attributes, patience.

It is apparent that as our faith matures, as we become closer to God, and as we seek His will instead of our own, that our patience grows. Unexpected obstacles in our paths just do not present issues that our previous outbursts may have suggested. We simply can wait, take a different path, or jump over the hurdle. It just is not quite as big a deal anymore.

I Found Him...watching a sparrow patiently wait for a rare snow to melt.

I FOUND HIM...STREET ENTERTAINER

IN A BIND? This street entertainer seems to have put himself into a bind. There seemingly is no way that he can escape from the cylinder. He's stuck!

I suspect that many of us also find ourselves in binds in which we see no logical way out. We're stuck. For the entertainer, there is indeed a way out, a trick that he performs several times daily. For us, however, it's not a "trick", it's for real. But no matter the bind, there is indeed a way out; even if it's not initially apparent.

Our way out is PRAYER. Psalms 138:3 tells us "When I pray, you answer me, and encourage me by giving me the strength that I need". In the same Psalm, verse 7 states "Though I am surrounded by troubles, you will bring me safely through them. You will clinch your fist against my enemies! Your power will save me." Humans are so stubborn sometimes. We get ourselves into situations that we try futilely to resolve on our own. The answer is right in front of us; shouting at us; slapping us in the face at times; but we do not see it, hear it, or feel it. The way out is FAITH! It's FAITH!

Sing His praises. Give thanks to His loving kindness. Ask Him for hope and for strength. There IS a way out—it starts with PRAYER.

I Found Him...while watching a street entertainer perform.

I FOUND HIM...LILY

Spring. What a wonderful season. Flowers bloom, dormant perennials magically reappear, cabin feverish weekend warriors emerge from their couches determined to turn their yard's To Do List into a To Done List. It's the season.

There are also seasons in our lives, from childhood to old age, offering unlimited opportunities. There are seasons for virtually everything in life. The lyrics for the hit song "Turn! Turn! Turn!" written by Peter Seeger, taken almost verbatim from Ecclesiastes and made famous by the Byrds in the 1960's says it beautifully. "A time to gain, a time to lose; A time to rend, a time to sew; A time to love, a time to hate; I time for love, a time for hate; A time for peace, I swear it's not too late".

There are seasons in our spiritual journey as well. The Lord tends to give us much responsibility, but never more than we can handle. The question is will we recognize His call and will we respond? It just may be the season to move in a new direction in your service to Him. Listen for it. Just as we adapt to the changing seasons in a year, we also will adapt to the changes that God is asking us to make.

Is it your season to shine, to emerge from a dormant state and blossom in His light?

I Found Him...in a beautiful lily bloom

I FOUND HIM...TRACK

I learned much observing Nicholas Sparks, the novelist, while he served as a volunteer high school track coach. He led his athletes to three consecutive state championships and set several national records.

First, contrary to conventional wisdom, he had very strenuous workouts on the days prior to routine meets. He explained that his team was focused on championships and setting national records. Lesson: have a clear vision.

Second, most track teams practice two to three months in the spring and not much more. His teams practiced year-round. Lesson: worthwhile goals require commitment.

Third, he stressed, even in workouts, to sprint through the finish line. Lesson: finish strong.

These lessons relate to everyday life. 1) We too need a vision; such as living a joyful, Christian life, as Paul speaks to in Romans 15. 2) Joy does not come naturally; it, like winning championships, requires commitment. How? By serving others; by Bible study; by prayer; by witnessing for God; by focusing on our blessings and thanking God for them daily; by always putting God first. 3) We too can finish strong by ALWAYS thriving to be Christ-like, being the hands of God, and living the faith. It is full-time and life-long.

God does not force us to put Him first; but He has given the invitation. He waits for our RSVP. Maybe now is the time to respond and to say YES to God.

I Found Him...while working-out at a high school track.

I Found Him…

I FOUND HIM...MOTHER'S DAY

Imagine the pain that Jesus' mother suffered. The physical pain of giving birth in a dirty stable, far from home. The anguish of hearing of plots to kill her son. The unimaginable horror watching at the foot of the cross. She indeed loved her son. And Jesus, at the cross in spite of His personal agony, "saw his mother and the disciple that He loved standing nearby and said 'Dear woman, here is your son' and to the disciple, 'Here is your mother.' From that time on the disciple took her into his home." John 19:26-27.

Mary showed great courage and obviously loved her son. Jesus, while suffering indescribable misery, arranged for the care of his mother.

Their love is a model for us all, unconditional love. Mothers make mistakes, children sometimes disappoint. Nevertheless, a mom's love perseveres and so does Jesus'. The lyrics of an old gospel song say "I'll be you father, I'll be your mother". As powerful as a mother's love is, Jesus' love is stronger.

Honor your mother today by accepting Jesus as your Lord. Mothers, honor your children by doing the same. He loves us as a woman loves her new-born child. He, like mothers, suffered for OUR discretions, but He is still willing to cradle us in His arms and love us—just like a loving mom.

Happy Mothers' Day!

I Found Him...watching a Black Neck Swan with her cygnet.

I FOUND HIM...DAYLILIES

Daylilies—beautiful daylilies! Just as other perennials, they lie dormant during the winter and reappear in the summer. The gorgeous blooms slowly close as darkness falls.

Many people seem to fall into a pattern similar to the daylily. At times they "bloom" in their love and work for the Lord, then retreat. They sometimes "lie dormant" for periods of time, and later reappear. Although this hot and cold approach to faith is better than no faith, it seems that a better approach is to start each day, each week, each year determined to love and serve the Lord.

We are reminded in Galatians 5:22 "But when the Holy Spirit controls our lives He will produce this kind of fruit in us: love, joy, peace, patience, kindness, goodness and self-control..." In observing people, are not those who exude peace and joy invariably those who serve the Lord EVERY day?

We therefore have two tasks: 1) live every day as God would have us to live, and 2) help those who have lost their way. Galatians 6:1-3 gives very clear instructions: "If a Christian is overcome by some sin, you who are godly should gently and humbly help him back onto the right path, remembering that next time it might be one of you who is in the wrong. Share each other's troubles and problems ... If anyone thinks that he is too great to stoop to this, he is fooling himself..."

I Found Him...in a spectacular daylily bloom.

I FOUND HIM...HORSE

"His pleasure is not in the strength of a horse, nor His delight in the legs of a man; the Lord delights in those that fear (*have reverence in*) Him, who put their hope in His unfailing love." (Psalm 147:10-11 NIV). How simple is that? Yet we as humans tend to complicate matters, overthink, or fail to think. When asked what the greatest commandment was, Jesus responded "Love the Lord your God with all your heart, all your soul (*being*), and all your mind..." (Matthew 22:37 NIV). It truly is just that simple; not easy, but simple.

A friend that I met through my work is an 88 year-old African-American lady living with her two daughters and a granddaughter in a small mobile home in the South. Her total worldly possessions consisted of a pair of slippers, two cotton house dresses, some underwear and minimal toiletries. I cannot imagine the hardships that this poverty-stricken woman experienced in her life. Yet she always spoke of how blessed she was, what a wonderful life that she had lead, and how God had been so good to her. This uneducated lady had great wisdom. She understood that His pleasure is not in the strength of a horse, nor was it in material possessions, wealth, or social status. She knew to put her hope in His unfailing love. Peace and contentment resulted.

I Found Him...as a magnificent horse exited a barn.

I FOUND HIM...OSPREY

Ospreys are a unique species of the hawk family in that their diet consists virtually of 100% live fish. They are great anglers, averaging a caught fish with only four dives, which usually takes only twelve minutes of hunting time. (Much better than my rate). Interestingly, at nest-building time, the male gathers twigs, small limbs, bark, vines, sod, etcetera and the female arranges it. (I'll leave that one alone). Each generation adds to the nest until they reach 3-6 feet diameters.

Spending time in nature, such as observing an osprey, marveling at their nests, and learning about their lifestyle is relaxing and invigorating. What a shame it is that many do it so rarely. Our fast-paced lives, centered on convenience, technology, and urbanization has taken us away from appreciating God's creation.

David wrote in Psalm 19:1-2 "The heavens declare the glory of God; the skies proclaim the work of His hands. Day after day they pour forth speech; night after night they display knowledge". David recognized that the Creator can be seen in His creation. I find that time spent away from man-made sounds, observing and listening, is a great way to grow closer to God. His awesomeness is exceedingly apparent and our holistic well-being is enhanced when we embrace the world of nature that surrounds us.

I Found Him...cautiously observing an osprey protect her nest.

I FOUND HIM...DAISY

A walk reveals so much if we will only look. A yard, a flower bed, several daisy plants, a single bloom of a daisy, and a bee feasting. If only the human eye could see beyond the bee. The beauty, and complexity, of God's creation is limitless. The psalmist writing Psalms 104 said it beautifully in verse 24: "Oh Lord, what a variety you have made! And in wisdom you have made them all! The earth is full of your riches".

This psalmist praises God for all of His creations; all of nature including plants, animals, mountains, the moon; everything. He emphasizes the dependency of all creatures on the Lord. Verses 27-28: "Every one of these depends on You to give them daily food. You supply it, and they gather it. You open wide your hand to feed them and they are satisfied with all your bountiful provision. But if You turn away from them, then all is lost..." He acknowledges the cycle of life. This daisy bloom will soon die and new life will emerge.

The powerful lesson is that, no matter how important that we think that we are, we too are dependent on God. He is the creator; He is the provider; He is the light of the world. Verse 33 states "I will sing to the Lord as long as I live. I will praise God to my last breath!"

I Found Him...with a hungry bee enjoying God's bounty.

I FOUND HIM...BRIGHT CLOUD

A bright cloud, pure white, stands out from the rest. Surrounded by sinister, ominous looking dark ones, it shines bright. Not unlike Christ Himself, who is the ultimate symbol of purity and righteousness, this cloud offers a reminder of the beauty of standing out from the crowd, and letting the light of Jesus shine through us.

We, just like this cloud formation, are ever changing. Each day we face new challenges, new situations, new hurdles as well as opportunities. The question is tough; will we fall back into the crowd, hide among the dark clouds, or will we have the courage to step away and shine?

Matthew 5:14-16 instructs us clearly: "You are the world's light—a city on a hill, glowing in the night for all to see. Don't hide your light! Let it shine for all; let your good deeds glow for all to see, so that they will praise your heavenly father."

Just as these clouds are constantly reshaping, God gives us the same opportunity. He allows us to wash away our sinful and broken ways, to reshape ourselves, to purify ourselves; all by His Grace. Come out from the dark clouds and shine brightly, confess your need for redemption through Jesus, and shout it to the world. Isaiah 60:1 "Arise my people! Let your light shine for all the nations to see! For the glory of the Lord is streaming from you."

I Found Him...standing out as a bright cloud.

I Found Him…

I FOUND HIM...STUMP

The remains of a once mighty tree peek out above the calm water, with only a hint of what once was. What is visible, though, is only a small part of the story. What is hidden is truly magnificent. A huge trunk, preserved in the sandy bottom; and a pristine root system woven deeply through the depths of the river floor exist, but are not seen.

Is not our relationship with God similar? We can feel and sense his presence; yet we allow Him to only show a fraction of who He is, of what He is, and what He COULD mean in our lives. We do have faith that He exists, but we do not dig deeper, uncover the awesomeness that is anxiously awaiting beneath the surface. We often do not dig through the sand and the muck to actually see what is there. Admittedly, it is not easy; but He is there for all who are willing to study, pray, and work to find Him; all of Him.

Dear Lord, You give us strength and hope every day. We feel Your presence daily, but there is so much more. Shove us into the depths of who You really are so that we can better understand You, better see the whole You, and better love and serve You. Graciously we pray, Amen.

I Found Him...in the slightly visible remains of a once towering tree.

I FOUND HIM...ABANDONED BOAT

An abandoned boat, rising and falling with the tide, subjected to continued weathering and beatings from storms, simply rots away.

Paul warns us in 1 Timothy 1:19 that there are people who have "shipwrecked" their faith by rejecting it. He describes those who disobey their consciences and deliberately do what they know is wrong. They sway with the wind as does this old boat. There is no anchor in their lives, no maintenance performed, indeed they have no direction. They need help, they need cleaning up and repairs; indeed, they need to be "towed" back to solid ground.

Are you a "shipwreck" needing repairs? Or maybe you know of someone who is. Christians are called to make disciples for Jesus Christ. The GREAT NEWS of the gospel is that no matter how rough we are, or how beaten down and abandoned that we feel; He will rescue us. He will make the repairs, clean away our past indiscretions, and put us back into service. The price for all this is simply FAITH.

Being a Christian has amazing benefits—peace, contentment, and salvation. There are obligations as well. The Great Commission in Matthew 28 tells us to "go and make disciples..." We are called to bring others to Jesus, to show them the way. The world today needs us to reach out to those who are "shipwrecked", and guide them to an abundant life in Jesus.

I Found Him...in the bow of an abandoned boat.

I FOUND HIM...SHACK

A sign posted on this structure says **"No Trespassing, Survivors Will Be Prosecuted"**. Someone obviously has a good sense of humor warning people to stay away from a dangerous place.

There is wisdom for our lives here as well. We all know people with whom we simply do not need to associate, who are dangerous. The Bible tells us "The righteous should CHOOSE HIS FRIENDS CAREFULLY, for the way of the wicked leads them astray." (Proverbs 12:26). And in 1 Corinthians 15:33-34, Paul says "Do not be misled: Bad company corrupts good character. Come back to your senses as you ought..." The message is clear: there are people, just like this dilapidated house, that we simply should avoid.

Once you truly enter into a walk with Jesus and your purpose is to honor Him, praise Him, and share the gospel; God will start pruning people from your lives that are dangerous and replace them with those who support and encourage your new life.

Our role is not to abandon those in need or those who struggle with their faith. For those we strive to provide the "maintenance" that they need to remain strong. There comes a time, however, just as with this crumbling shed, that they are too dangerous and we need to move on. "He who walks with wise men will be wise, but the companion of fools will be destroyed." (Proverbs 13:20).

I Found Him...in the deteriorated ruins of a neglected house.

I FOUND HIM…SALAMANDER

A salamander, scurrying on his hunt, changes colors to match his surroundings. Camouflaged brown meandering through the dried pine straw will change to green shortly as he moves into a green shrub. The ploy is to go unnoticed as he instinctively changes with the environment, rendering it virtuously impossible to definitively identify his true color.

Are we not oftentimes like a salamander? While in church we are one color. The night before, however, we were a different color, at work another, and with friends, yet another.

David prayed in Psalm 26 "For I have taken Your loving kindness and Your truth as my ideals. I do not have fellowship with tricky, two-faced men; they are false and hypocritical….I publically praise the Lord for keeping me from slipping and falling." And in Matthew 23:25-26, Jesus tells the religious leaders that "you are so careful to polish the outside of the cup, but the inside is foul with extortion and greed…First clean the inside of the cup, and then the whole cup will be clean."

Those who truly love the Lord, who proclaim Him to be their rock, and are guided daily by His love, His truth, and His grace; stand out. They are easy to spot. Regardless of their surroundings, their smiles shout, their manner illuminates, their peacefulness glows. There is no need to change colors, they love God; everywhere and always.

I Found Him…watching colors change on the back of a busy salamander.

I FOUND HIM...HORNETS' NEST

I accidently and literally "stirred up a hornets' nest" while trimming a bush in the backyard; and I was stung. These hornets worked tirelessly building their home and never bothered me until I poked around somewhere that I should not have been.

People sometimes have a knack for this when they allow themselves to gossip. We spread rumors, repeat negative stories, or simply talk to tear down instead of building up. Why? How can such actions possibly help us? Psychiatrists and those more learned than me can answer that; but it appears to show a character flaw in the gossipers. They somehow feel that they are more important if they can make someone else look bad.

Proverbs 6:16-19 states that "the Lord hates...Sowing discord among brothers". Ephesians 4:29 confirms: "Let no corrupting talk come out of your mouths, but only such as is good for building up, as fits the occasion, that it may give grace to those who hear". Psalm 34:13 says: "Keep your tongue from evil and your lips from speaking deceit". These and numerous other Bible references make it clear; this is NOT the way of the Lord. Yet we do it.

I learned the hard way to stay clear of a hornet's nest. Maybe we all can learn to simply stay clear of others who seem to enjoy "stirring up the hornet's nest". It may just save us the misery of being stung.

I Found Him...in a hornets' nest.

I FOUND HIM...DILAPIDATED HOUSE

Imagine this house back in the day. It had character, was functional, and certainly was a place where memories were made. It started deteriorating when routine maintenance stopped. Without managing the small issues, the house declined steadily to the point where it was no longer salvageable.

Many times we too need help, call it routine maintenance. The problem/issue may not be huge, but it needs addressing. Unfortunately, we often do not seek nor will we accept help. Pride get in the way. Proverbs 11:2 "When pride comes in, then comes disgrace, but with humility comes wisdom". We hide behind a false sense of self-confidence that actually is self-deception. Paul tells us in Galatians 6:2 to "Carry each other's burdens and in this way you will fulfill the law of Christ". It seems easier at times to help someone else than it is to ask for or even accept help from others. The fact is, however, that we all need help. Situations arise when we simply need a helping hand; someone to "carry our burden".

Just as this house did not receive the necessary help when its issues were small, we too can find the weight of our problems increasing to the point that we cave in like this roof. Start now; seek help when needed, perform the necessary maintenance. First by asking the Lord, and then, by swallowing your pride and accepting assistance from others.

I Found Him...as a once beautiful home weathers away.

I FOUND HIM...FLAMINGO

Although this flamingo has a perfectly good reason to have his head under water (fishing); doesn't this image speak volumes about so many people that we know?

Many people "bury their heads", refusing to see the obvious. God's love, peace and grace are everywhere. He is in the sparkling eyes of a toddler; in the quiet smile of a homeless shelter volunteer; in the comforting peace on the face of a believer, in the enthusiastic step of a lost soul who has now found the Lord. He is directly in front of us, yet we as humans sometimes are simply too stubborn to see.

Psalms 4:7 says it clearly. "Yes, the gladness You have given me is far greater than their joys at harvest time..." The life of a true believer is amazing; and is available to all. No matter the circumstance, no matter how bleak life seems; there is hope, there is a better way, and there is joy and contentment awaiting. The answer is simple; not easy, but simple. It is God. He will carry the load. In all things, praise Him. Serve Him. Take your head out of the water, raise it high, and proclaim to the world: "The Lord is alive and well, living in me". He is here for us; if we will only reach out and grab Him.

I Found Him ...in the image of a fishing flamingo.

I FOUND HIM...ABANDONED CHURCH

This picture is used symbolically since I do not know the history of this particular church; but it does seem that many churches are dying. The congregations are rapidly aging, attendance is declining, and many church goers are becoming complacent.

One factor affecting the decline of churches may also be an issue for people in general; we often are too inwardly focused. The Bible teaches love. Mother Teresa once told this story: "I picked up a man from the street, and he was eaten alive from worms. Nobody could stand him, and he was smelling so badly. I went to him, and he asked, 'Why do you do this?' I said, 'Because I love you.'" Jesus made it very clear in Matthew 25:45 when he said "Truly I tell you, whatever you did not do for one of the least of these, you did not do for me."

The message is clear, to love Jesus is to love everyone. When a church's focus is inside the church walls, or when we as individuals focus on ourselves, we fall into a downwardly spiraling trap. (This certainly does not imply to ignore one's own health or the church facilities). The emphasis, however, needs to be on others; to look for their positive traits, to celebrate them and to reach out to them. It is ironic that outwardly focused churches and individuals who serve God by helping others, are richly blessed themselves.

I Found Him...in a dilapidated shell of a once vibrant church.

I FOUND HIM...BOYCE

Boyce, a single teacher, was facing a Thanksgiving alone — his family 2,500 miles away. So, we invited him to celebrate the day with our family. Within minutes of arriving, he was in the den with the children, laughing, rolling on the floor, and enjoying life.

The following spring, Boyce, struggling to pronounce his words, had to focus intently to complete a sentence. He resorted to using a microphone in his classroom, simply trying to communicate. The diagnosis came soon: ALS (Lou Gehrig's disease). His condition deteriorated rapidly, but he continued to communicate with friends via email. I vividly remember his last email: It started with: "I'm having a great day. I hope that you are." He described his physical condition: he no longer could walk, he no longer could talk; he could barely raise one finger to slowly-- and meticulously-- type that email. Yet Boyce was having a great day.

I have noticed that Boyce, and others who are bubbling over with joy, peace, and contentment, who have a passion for life regardless of the situation, have a common thread. They each share an unwavering faith in, and have a personal relationship with, our Lord and Savior, Jesus Christ. The joy that we so desperately seek is available to all, regardless of our situations, through faith. Although elusive, it truly is just that simple, FAITH.

I'm having a great day; I hope that you are.

I Found Him... in an E-mail from my friend, Boyce.

I FOUND HIM...SUNRISE

A new day dawns—opportunities abound! What will we do with it? Those struggling with relationships, with family, at work, or with life in general; now is the time to ask: Is this how I want to live? Life is about choices, and although it is tough to see sometimes, there are alternatives. It truly is up to us to make the conscience decision to live differently, to change directions. It is about a new attitude. This new day offers just that opportunity.

Consider the message from Deuteronomy 30:19-20 "I call heaven and earth to witness against you that today I have set before you life or death, blessing or curse. Oh, that you will choose life; that you and your children might live. Choose to love the Lord your God and obey Him and cling to Him; for He is your life and the length of your days."

The first step is to simply trust in the Lord. Resolve that: "no, I will not live like this anymore." Ask for His guidance and make the necessary changes that He shows you. Admittedly, this is easier said than done. Remember, though, that you are not alone. You have the unlimited power and strength of our Lord on which to lean. He will guide you, support you, and help you; but only if YOU decide to change your ways and SINCERELY strive to follow Him.

I Found Him...admiring, in awe, a new day emerge.

I FOUND HIM...LONE TREE

Alone tree, different, apart, isolated; not able to adapt to an eroding shoreline, withers away. Many people relate to this tree. They too feel isolated, alone, with a figurative sea of water preventing healthy relationships and companionships. They too, feel as if they are withering with no escape.

THERE IS HOPE! The power of Almighty God is here, available, and wanting to help. The strength of the Holy Spirit can lift you off of the island and place you on firm ground. Isaiah 41:10 reassures us with the words: "Fear not, for I am with you. Do not be dismayed. I am your God. I will strengthen you; I will help you; I will uphold you with my victorious right hand."

Put your faith in Him. Start today, moving toward shore, one step at a time; one conversation at a time; one kind deed at a time. Know that He is guiding you, directing you, and protecting you. Listen to Him. Oh what a wonderful feeling it is to know that in God's eyes; you are important, you are wanted, you are loved.

Psalms 118:5-6 also gives us strength and courage: "In my distress I prayed to the Lord and He answered me and rescued me. He is for me. How can I be afraid? What can mere man do to me?" Call on Him today-He WILL respond.

I Found Him...in an isolated tree overtaken by changing times.

I FOUND HIM...COTTON FIELD

A nother season rapidly comes to an end. This beautiful field of cotton emerged after a summer's work and soon will be harvested. The cycle continues-new life, new beginnings, and new opportunities.

Our walk with Christ is similar. As we nurture our relationship with Him, work on discerning His will, and confess our sins to Him; He washes our slate clean and we are figuratively cleansed as white as this mature cotton. We can start again with the purity of a freshly plowed field. 2 Corinthians 5:17 explains it this way: "Therefore, if anyone is in Christ, he is a new creature; the old has gone, the new has come!"

The farmer tending to this cotton will soon reap the benefits of a long, hard spring and summer of preparing for a new crop, planting it, caring for it, and finally harvesting and selling it. Maybe it is time for us to begin anew with God. Certainly we have stumbled, surely we have strayed, but the beauty of Jesus is that there is always another opportunity; another season awaits. 2 Corinthians 5:21 offers this assurance: "God made Him who had no sin, so that in Him we might become the righteousness of God". We too can bear fruit as pure as this white cotton. Let's start now with a new season of LOVING the LORD.

I Found Him...on a beautiful cotton farm

I FOUND HIM...BANDED DUCK

Take a close look at this wild duck. He has a band on his leg enabling wildlife personnel to track him and gather much pertinent data. Today, smart phones, tablets, even cameras and other devices have built-in GPS devices allowing us to be tracked as well. This amazing technology offers many advantages, but it also is a little scary not knowing if someone is following us.

If we look at the bigger picture, however, these man-made devices pale in comparison to the Lord's "tracking system" that has been in place for all of time. Paul reminds us in Romans 14: 11-12 "It is written, 'As surely as I live, says the Lord, every knee will bow before me; every tongue will confess to God.' So then, each of us will give an account of himself to God." It reminds me of the song regarding Santa "He knows if you've been good or bad, so be good for goodness sake".

The Holy Spirit is with us always, ready and able to help fight our sinful nature. It is up to us to solicit His help. Knowing that we are accountable for our actions, that indeed there is a "tracking system" built into us, helps. The Holy Spirit will, working through our conscience, guide us. Just as scientists learn from banding wildlife, we are motivated knowing that the Lord has "banded" us.

I Found Him...watching mallards enjoy a sunny day.

I FOUND HIM...TURTLE

A turtle stretches out from his protective shell, seemingly enjoying the sun and a beautiful day. By leaving the safety and comfort of his shell, he experiences life. We too have our own comfort zones, "shells", which provide us protection; but just like the turtle, look at what we miss by not venturing out.

The Lord wants us to stretch ourselves, to live in ways that are often against our nature. He asks us not to take the easy path, not to succumb to comfortable, worldly ways, but to indeed become a "Living Sacrifice" for Him. Paul urges us in Romans 12: 2: "Do not conform any longer to the pattern of this world, but be transformed by the renewing of your mind. Then you will be able to test and approve what God's will is---His good, pleasing and perfect will." To be transformed means to always pray; to study the Bible, to be joyful; to always be thankful. It means to follow the Holy Spirit, not our natural sinful ways. A transformed person lacks greed, does not seek excuses for sin, associates with Godly people, and has the courage to stretch out from his/her comforting shells.

It is ironic that those who are transformed, those that do not conform, and those that truly follow the Holy Spirit outside of their comfort zones learn and appreciate how His ways are truly satisfying.

I Found Him...with a stretched out turtle basking in the sun.

I FOUND HIM...WEEDS

Focused on the weeds and missing what is truly important? Great leaders in business, government, or other organizations know the importance of a clear-cut vision. Their role often times is one of sharing the vision, over and over, with every member of the organization. For how can an organization move forward if 1) all within it do not know where they are going and 2) all are not working together toward a common goal? A huge mistake many leaders make is that they are reactive rather than proactive. They get caught up in the "weeds" and lose track of the bigger picture. They fail to strive to reach their vision because they are side-tracked by day-to-day challenges or simply do not know or understand the vision.

Is it not the same in our individual lives? We are so consumed with making it through the day that we forget our real purpose. We do not know nor do we seek to understand our vision, where we are headed. We fail to constantly move toward Christ. The Living Bible paraphrases Psalms 119: 18-19 this way: "Open my eyes to see the wonderful things in your Word. I am but a pilgrim here on earth: how I need a map—and your commands are my chart and guide."

It is time for many of us to open our eyes, see the obvious, and set our sight, our energy, and our resolve on following the "map", Jesus.

I Found Him...in a field of weeds.

I FOUND HIM...EAGLE'S WINGS

A juvenile Bald Eagle soars seemingly with little effort on a crisp fall morning, sparking images of strength, power, and determination. Driven close to extinction years ago by DDT poisoning and illegal killing, this magnificent creature once again thrives and inspires, just as it did in Biblical days.

The prophet Isaiah, centuries before Christ, wrote of eagles to make a powerful point. In Isaiah 40:28-31 he writes "...The Lord is the everlasting God, the Creator of the ends of the earth. He will not grow tired or weary, and His understanding no one can fathom. He gives strength to the weary and increases the power of the weak. Even youths grow tired and weary, and young men stumble and fall; but those who hope in the Lord will renew their strength. They will soar on wings like eagles; they will run and not grow weary, they will walk and not be faint".

Although the message is certainly easier said than done, it is a most uplifting one. Trust the Lord. Put your hope in Him. Love Him. Have FAITH! Those doing so enjoy renewed spiritual strength, an energized will to serve, and a refreshing excitement for life. Isaiah continues in Isaiah 41:10 "So do not fear, for I am with you; do not be dismayed. For I am your God".

So soar on wings like eagles; the Lord's wings.

I Found Him...observing a young eagle making his daily rounds.

I FOUND HIM...GRAPE VINE

For this bee, I suspect that life simply does not get any better than this. Oh the sweet taste of a ripe muscadine grape! This vine bears luscious fruit, year after year, with the help of nurturing hands that fertilize it, prune it, and generally work on it.

We too can bear fruit; fruit even more delicious than these juicy grapes. Paul explains in Galatians 5:22 that those who allow the Holy Spirit to guide their lives will also bear fruit. He identifies the Fruit of the Spirit as love, joy, peace, patience, kindness, goodness, faithfulness, gentleness, and self-control. We as a people are spiritually hungry. Society has taught many to worship money, power, prestige and other superficialities. It is the role of Christians, through faith, to work hard to produce fruit; fruit as described in Galatians. This feeds those starving for meaning, those hungering for peace and contentment; and those engulfed in consumerism.

Just as this grape vine requires much attention, so does our walk with Christ. We fertilize and prune through prayer, study, small groups learning and sharing together, church, and simply associating with other Christians.

We too can enjoy the fruits of our faith. To love God and to serve Him requires effort; it does not grow without nurturing. Peace and contentment is available to all, though, regardless of the past, through faith. It simply needs nurturing.

I Found Him...in a muscadine grape vine.

I FOUND HIM...PILE OF JUNK

Wow, what a mess! As we start another new year, many plan to tidy up, get things back in order, and get organized for the upcoming year. Even if our residences or work spaces are not quite as disheveled as the one pictured, we sometimes feel as if our lives are in disarray just as this abandoned house.

The bible references disorder numerous times. In 1 Corinthians 14:33 Paul writes of the importance of an orderly worship service: "For God is not a God of disorder but of peace". In 2 Corinthians 12:20 Paul writes "For I am afraid that when I come that I may not find you as I want you to be...I fear that there will be quarrelling, jealousy, outbursts of anger, factions, slander, gossip, arrogance and disorder." Finally in James 3:16, James writes "For where you have envy and selfish ambition, there you find disorder and every evil practice."

It is clear that God wants to be worshipped in an orderly fashion so as not to discredit Him. It also seems that He wants us to live uncluttered lives; lives focused on Him; serving Him, pleasing Him, and worshipping Him.

So as we start a new year committed to reorganizing our households and putting "things" in order; let us also resolve to put our lives in order, to unclutter our thoughts, and most importantly, to focus on Him.

I Found Him...in a pile of junk in an abandoned house.

I FOUND HIM...HERON

A Tricolored Heron, sunning on a pier, apparently has an itch; so he scratches it. His itch is a pretty insignificant part of his day just as one is for us. There are other itches that we have, however, that are not as insignificant.

God calls us in many ways. It sometimes starts out as a feeling, or an uneasiness, or maybe just a thought; all seemingly as insignificant as a minor itch. Ignoring it, however, does not seem to work. God continues to call, even if we do not immediately act. It's still there. For some, the "itch" continues to grow. The call becomes louder, starts to take up more of our conscience time, and simply will not go away. Hallelujah!

Our challenge, is first to discern His will. Through prayer, reflection, and study, His will emerges. The Living Bible paraphrases Romans 12:2 this way: "Don't copy the behavior and customs of this world, but be a new and different person with a fresh newness in all you do and think. Then you will learn from your own experience how His ways will really satisfy you".

The lesson is to not ignore God's will; SEEK it. Listen for it, look for it, find it, and then scratch it. "His ways will really satisfy you". Following Him is indeed the way, the light, and the truth. When you feel Him tugging, pray "Thy will be done".

I Found Him...watching a heron scratch an itch.

I FOUND HIM...HISTORIC FARM

This recently taken photograph depicts a lifestyle from a bygone era. I see children doing chores before school; a farmer up before sunrise tackling never ending tasks and in bed shortly after sunset. I can almost smell fresh food devoured with vigor, all grown and prepared on site. I see several generations learning values, nurturing the land, raising families, and reaping harvests from honest, dedicated toil.

Life is different today; but the lessons learned certainly still apply. The value of honest hard work, no short-cuts, setting priorities, and appreciating what we have; never changes.

Our responsibility to love, serve, and work in God's Kingdom also remains unchanged. The manner in which we reach people may be different with technology, as is worship styles; but the message of hope remains clear, applicable, unchanged, and vital. The relationship with our Lord also requires hard work and a steadfast resolve to nurture it all day, every day.

Take a moment to reflect to a time imagined in this picture. Also, think of Paul's words to the Thessalonians when he said that "we are not trying to please people, but we are trying to please God..." It may be time to set new priorities, to focus on pleasing God, and commit to the hard work that this requires. You too will reap a bountiful harvest.

I Found Him...on a beautiful farm from yesteryear.

I FOUND HIM......THANKSGIVING

Happy Thanksgiving All! This is just a short note to suggest that you take a moment, take a deep breath, and picture yourself in a simpler time. Maybe think of a time like the family in this house must have had at Thanksgiving. Once you have cleared your mind of the clutter of Black Friday, the stress and the hustle/bustle of the holidays, stop and truly THANK GOD.

Most importantly, thank God for His son and our savior, Jesus Christ. What better gift is there than to know that, through faith, we are saved? Regardless of our situation, our past, or suffering that we have endured, Jesus paid the price for us. Our sins are forgiven and salvation awaits. We did not earn it, but it is ours nevertheless—through faith. Thank God.

As Paul instructed in 1Thessalonians 5:16-18 "Rejoice always, pray continually, give thanks in all circumstances; for this is God's will for you in Christ Jesus."

Let's make EVERYDAY, Thanksgiving Day!

I Found Him…while contemplating a simpler time.

I Found Him…

Winter

I FOUND HIM...PELICANS

Two pelicans, in the middle of a changing, flowing, and uncertain river, found something solid on which to cling; old pilings anchored deeply in the sand. The birds are content, relying on their sturdy perches to keep from drifting.

We too battle a strong current. Paul explains to us in Romans 7:13-25 how humans are born with the power of sin within us. He describes our struggle with human nature pulling us toward sin while our conscience and our mind pull back. We want to do what is right, we try, but for some reason we simply cannot always do so. It is exhausting and frankly, impossible without help.

These pelicans found help staying stationary in the current, without which they too would be exhausted. The power of sin, similar to the birds' dilemma battling a flowing river, is simply too much for us to battle on our own. Paul offers hope to combat what some refer to as being slaves to sin. Jesus Christ! Yes, Jesus is the piling on which we can cling. When we are exhausted from "swimming upstream", we can perch on the strong shoulders of Jesus. Paul says it best in Romans 7:24-25 "What a wretched man I am! Who will rescue me from this body of death? Thanks be to God—through Jesus Christ our Lord!" Thanks be to God indeed.

I Found Him...watching contented, sunning pelicans.

I FOUND HIM...CYPRESS TREE

As I looked at this decaying house, I also thought of the life of this cypress tree. Starting as a seed, vulnerable to its environment, one of many that spouted; it grew into a flexible sapling, adapting to the conditions of the day. It grew stronger through the years, withstanding violent storms, floods, droughts, ice storms, heat waves, and human abuse. But it withstood the trials and now stands tall, valiantly guarding this once stately farm house that it has outlived.

Is this tree's journey not symbolically similar to ours? We are born into this world, helpless, dependent, and a product of chance. We did not choose our parents nor did we dictate their ability to raise a child. We did not ask to be brought into this world; but we were. We survived and grew, somehow.

Now, though, WE make choices. We can 1) go it alone, rigid in our thoughts, and face the "storms" of our lives with a false sense of strength. Those choosing this route seem to "snap in the wind". The other choice is 2) to give ourselves to God who allows us the flexibility to sway with the wind, to continue to learn and grow while staying grounded with deep roots; roots of a love and passion to serve Him.

I Found Him... in the swaying limbs of an aging cypress tree.

I FOUND HIM...SWANS

Tundra Swans, flying in perfect formation, rely on each other to make their 4,000 mile semi-annual trip from Alaska/Canada to eastern North Carolina and back. Traveling in flocks, with family members together, they soar at 50 mph+ two miles high. They minimize their energy use by positioning themselves and coordinating their wing beats perfectly with the others.

The Bible offers similar advice regarding working together. Ecclesiastes 4:9-12 for example, says "Two are better than one, because they have good return for their work. If one falls down, his friend can help him up! Also, if two lie down together, they will keep warm. But how can one keep warm alone? Though one may be overpowered, two can defend themselves. A cord of three strands is not quickly broken."

The point is that we are not alone. The Bible instructs family, friends or even strangers to help one another. Joining together to help is a trait that exists in humans just as it does with these swans. It sometimes gets lost in the nightly news, and we may have to be a little more intentional to make it a daily habit, but the instinct is there.

Just as God extends His loving hands to help us, let us also extend our hands to others. Together we better serve and love the Lord; and together we can positively change our lives and the world.

I Found Him...while gazing at majestic swans soaring overhead.

I FOUND HIM...ABANDONED HOUSE

Oh what memories this house could share! The pig-pickings, Thanksgivings, Christmases, spring plantings and fall harvests, Sunday dinners, good times and bad, long hours farming and sweet Sunday rests all appear to fade away. This once stately farm house served proudly, but it cannot last forever. Time takes its toll.

God's love and grace, on the other hand, is timeless. In John 15:16, Jesus speaks to His disciples "You did not choose me, but I chose you to go and bear fruit – fruit that will last". This fruit has indeed lasted, 2,000+ years and counting. Unlike man-made structures, this fruit lasts because it is from the Spirit of the living God. Paul explains in 2 Corinthians 3:3 "You show that you are a letter from Christ, the result of our ministry, written not in ink but with the Spirit of the living God, not on tablets of stone, but on tablets of human hearts". God's grace continues to live in our hearts.

So even as magnificent as this house once was, it lasts only a finite time. In contrast to this, God's grace, (an undeserved gift and unearned love of God through the Holy Spirit) stays with us forever as we strive to further develop a relationship with Him.

Lord, we thank you for your timeless grace, that as years defeat earthly objects, You remain strong; our rock, our hope. In Jesus name we pray. Amen

I Found Him...in an abandoned old farm house.

I FOUND HIM...GREAT EGRET

On a cold wintry morning, shortly after sunrise, I was mesmerized by thousands of swans, geese, ducks, and other migratory wildlife wintering near a local lake. The sounds of thousands of birds honking seemed poetic. This Great Egret indeed was poetry in motion as it gracefully glided over the marsh. This picture sparks an overwhelming feeling of praise and astonishment due to the beauty of God's creation. It mysteriously leads me to the glorious poetry in Psalms.

Psalm 136: 1-2, 4--9 and 25-26 represents a liturgy of praise to the Lord as Creator. "Give thanks to the Lord, for He is good. *His love endures forever*. Give thanks to the God of Gods. *His love endures forever*. To Him who alone does great wonders, *His love endures forever*; who by His understanding made the heavens, *His love endures forever*; who spread out the earth upon the waters, *His love endures forever*; who made the great lights, *His love endures forever*; the sun to govern the day, *His love endures forever*; the moon and the stars to govern the night, *His love endures forever*...and who gives food to every creature, *His love endures forever*. Give thanks to the God of heaven.   *His love endures forever*."

God is with us! His creation is bubbling over with wonder. Stop, take a deep breath, look and listen for the poetry that is God's Creation. Thanks be to God.

I Found Him...as a Great Egret slowly skimmed over pristine marshland.

I FOUND HIM...FISHING BOAT

Work boats, not show boats, sit in the harbor after a long day at sea. These are "work horses", obviously not for show. Their strength lies in functionality, getting the job done, silently working day after day. They certainly do not get the attention that similarly sized luxury yachts receive, but they are steady, reliable, and perform their duties tirelessly.

We all know people in organizations who are the "Show Boats"; and we also know those who quietly perform the necessary work in the background, not seeking recognition or glory. They simply get the job done.

We are reminded often throughout the Bible that the Lord favors those who are genuine, who work for His Kingdom, not their own. We are called to do so, for Him, not for us. Jeremiah 48:10 warns us this way: "A curse on him who is lax in doing the Lord's work..." Jesus explained to us in John 9:4 "As long as it is day, we must do the work of him who sent me. Night is coming, when no one can work."

Show boat or work boat, which are we? And which one does God prefer us to be? As difficult as it is for humans, it is clear that God expects us to be His hands and feet. We are to serve Him and to glorify Him; certainly not us.

I Found Him...on a pier with docked fishing boats.

I FOUND HIM...CORMORANT

Double-breasted Cormorants, from a distance, are dark, gangly, prehistoric-looking birds with snaky necks. I was shocked when I processed this picture to see what a gorgeous creature it actually is. They possess quite colorful orange-yellow skin around its beak, a symmetrical pattern along its back, and sparking aquamarine eyes that shine like jewels.

This picture reminded me of how many people who, from a distance, appear to be something different than they actually are. We are often too quick to judge based solely on first impressions and/or appearances. If we get "closer", we realize that there truly is a beautiful person hidden behind the outer shell.

Psalms 7:8 asks God to "Judge me, O Lord, according to my righteousness, according to my integrity". And Jesus is very specific in John 7:24 when He says: "Stop judging by mere appearances, and make a right judgment." It is clear that everyone is a child of God and that each is beautiful in their unique way. The beauty emerges when we look for it. Although ones appearance, skin color, hair style, clothes, and other outwardly features sometimes indicate of who the person is, we really do not know until we "snap the shutter" and study the details. A jewel may be hidden underneath a deceiving façade.

The old saying "You can't judge a book by looking at its cover" certainly applies. Abandon stereotypes and find jewels.

I Found Him...in an image of a surprisingly pretty aquatic bird

I FOUND HIM...COUNTRY STORE

A once vibrant country store, a destination where people gathered to share stories, enjoy a sense of community, and obtain needed supplies; now is abandoned and overtaken by the aggressive onslaught of relentless weeds and briars. Indifference allowed the weeds' dominance.

The same applies to us. Paul tells us in Romans 7:5 "For when we are controlled by the sinful nature, the sinful passions aroused by the law were at work in our bodies so that we bore fruit for death." It is the nature of humans to sin. From the time of Adam, humans innately desire the forbidden; and it is a powerful force. Left unattended, as are the weeds engulfing this old store, sin and death will also engulf us.

Our sinful nature is no excuse and is not permission for sin to overtake us. Through the Holy Spirit we are able to repent and intentionally decide to follow Christ. It is through our failures that the Spirit gives us strength to fight back, to cut out the weeds in our lives, and to allow Christ to help us battle our sinful nature.

The choice is clear: 1) do the maintenance daily, live in the Spirit, love and follow Christ and enjoy life and peace; or 2) give in to the sinful nature which leads to hostility with God and spiritual death.

I Found Him... at an abandoned country store overtaken by weeds.

I FOUND HIM...GULL ON ICE

A Ring-billed gull stands confidently on very thin ice. I suspect that he knows the tenuous nature of his perch and is prepared for its melting, however.

Many of us are figuratively standing on thin ice. We seem to succumb to our sinful nature and through our actions show the world what is in our hearts. We mistakenly confuse God's patience with a convenient thought that He is not concerned with our sinful ways. This is a scary mistake.

Paul warns us emphatically in Romans 2:5 that "...because of your stubbornness and unrepentant heart, you are storing up wrath against yourself for the day of God's wrath, when His righteous judgment will be revealed. God will give to each person according to what he has done." Oh my! Are we ready to receive what we deserve? Paul is clear that we cannot work our way into heaven, but based on the above, he also is clear that what is important is what is in our hearts.

God is indeed patient and it is through this patience that He leads people to repentance. (Romans 2:4). He also judges us with absolute justice. He is indeed impartial, judging us on deeds and motives. He does not show favorites (Romans 2:11).

The time is now, before the "ice melts", to repent (to change one's mind or to make a decisive turn). God is calling us to change our hearts.

I Found Him...with a gull on thin ice.

I FOUND HIM...MOON

The moon shines brightly over the eastern sky, illuminating the otherwise darkness of the night. Sailors and explorers have navigated the world for centuries solely by using the moon and the stars. They set their direction by the alignment of the stars and moon. Although it is not easy, they strive to first set a direction and next, follow it.

It appears that far too many people go through life with no direction. They have no North Star, no moon, nothing to guide them. They simply are rowing their boats in circles.

A better way, indeed the only way, to set a course in your life is to look to the skies and follow God. Jesus said in John 8:12 "I am the Light of the world. So if you follow me, you won't be stumbling through the darkness, for living light will flood your path."

Certainly there are many obstacles that get in the way, that make it easy to get off course. Our challenge is to fight through these hurdles, push them aside, and stay the course. Love Him, praise Him, worship Him, and FOLLOW Him. He is the moon and the stars by which we navigate. He is our compass. He will indeed show you the way; if you will just believe, ask Him for guidance, and follow His direction.

I Found Him...while admiring a magnificent "super moon".

Jeff Jenkins

I FOUND HIM... TWO TUNDRA SWANS

Tundra swans are absolutely fascinating creatures. Not only do they work together to migrate from Alaska to the east coast and back every year; they also, after a one-year "courtship", mate for life (ten to twenty years).

We certainly can learn about teamwork and helping one another from them. We can also learn a great lesson regarding loyalty.

Their dedication to their mate speaks not only to our human relationships, but also to our relationship with God. Should not our loyalty to God be as strong as that of two swans? Jesus tells us in Matthew 22:37-38 "You must love the Lord your God with all your heart, with all you being, and with all your mind. This is the first and greatest commandment." Paul is adamant about our love for God. When we love God this purely, everything that we do, everywhere, is intended to please Him. We will WANT to follow His path, not ours. He too has pledged His love for us. Hebrews 13:5 tells us that God has said: "Never will I leave you; never will I forsake you." Deuteronomy 31:6 affirms this by saying that God will "never leave you nor forsake you."

God's creation offers powerful life lessons if we will only look. The lifelong family of two swans inspires us in our worldly relationships, and it reinforces the ultimate loyalty-the mutual love we share with God.

I Found Him... as a pair of swans flew by.

I FOUND HIM...HUNKERED DOWN PELICAN

On a frigid, windy day, a pelican hunkers down, as if anchored, unbothered by the bone chilling gusts that are penetrating this photographer. The bird seems perfectly prepared and thus unaffected by the fierce conditions. The Lord has provided him with the means to persevere.

We too have a means to become anchored, unaffected by the "winds" of our society. The Lord also provides for us, prepares us, and allows us a means to flourish. We, just as the pelican, must intentionally use the gifts and tools that the Lord provides.

James tells us in James 1:1-3 to "Consider it pure joy, my brothers, whenever you face trails of many kinds, because you know that the testing of your faith develops perseverance". He continues in verses 5-6 "If any of you lack wisdom, he should ask God, who gives generously to all without finding fault, and it will be given to him. But when he asks, he must believe and not doubt, because he who doubts is like a wave in the sea, blown and tossed by the wind".

This world seems overwhelming at times with powerful obstacles "tossing us in the wind". Faith, however, is our anchor. Faith is the warm feathers protecting us. Faith is indeed our hope and means to persevere.

Thanks be to God!

I Found Him...while shivering trying to photograph a contented pelican.

I FOUND HIM...CHRISTMAS TREE

Take a close look; it is a Christmas tree with all of the glitter, glitz, and electricity that has become so common in American homes. Look closer to see a symbol of the greatest gift of all time, the cross.

The chorus of "The Perfect Tree", a hymn written by Ray Boltz, seems apropos. "The perfect tree Grew long ago And it was not decked with silver Or with ornaments of gold. But hanging from its branches Was a gift for you and me. Jesus laid His life down On the perfect tree".

I am blessed to have given and received gifts today, all neatly wrapped under the tree. Without diminishing the love that these earthly gifts represent, none compares to the gift that God gave to us; the gift of Jesus, who He sent to earth on this day centuries ago.

Paul tells us in Romans 8:38-39 that neither death or life, the power in hell, our fears or our worries; no matter where we are, that nothing will separate us from the love of God demonstrated by our Lord Jesus Christ when he died for us.

As you celebrate, open presents and look at a Christmas tree today, see Jesus. See Him on the cross and thank Him for the greatest gift imaginable; His promise of salvation for all who believe in Him. We honor His birth today!

I Found Him ... staring deeply into a "Perfect" Christmas tree.

BIBLE QUOTES

All of the Bible quotes, unless otherwise noted, are from The NIV Study Bible.

PHOTOGRAPHY CREDITS

The photography in this book, including the cover, were taken by the author (with the exception of those of Mr. Gire. Those were provided by his family).

ABOUT THE AUTHOR

Jeff Jenkins, a life-long United Methodist, currently serves as a United Methodist District Lay Leader where he works with eighty-four churches to empower, motivate, and train laity to reach out to make disciples for Jesus Christ.

Mr. Jenkins is a University of North Carolina-Chapel Hill MBA who enjoyed a career in retail management and consulting and was a managing partner in a residential building and development company.

He and his wife Bedie have two grown children, Jay and Leigh.

He enjoys photography, water skiing, running and taking courses of all kinds. He is rejuvenated weekly by writing and posting to his Facebook Ministry www.Facebook.com/IFoundHimMinistry.

Made in the USA
Middletown, DE
25 November 2015